W9-AVL-853

The Museum of PHOBIAS

The HARROWING HUMAN Gallery

By JOHN WOOD AND DANIELLE JONES

Gareth Stevens
PUBLISHING

Rocky River Public Library

Please visit our website, www.garethstevens.com.
For a free color catalog of all our high-quality books,
call toll free 1-800-542-2595 or fax 1-877-542-2596.

Cataloging-in-Publication Data

Names: Wood, John. | Jones, Danielle.
Title: The harrowing human gallery / John Wood and Danielle
Jones.
Description: New York : Gareth Stevens Publishing, 2021. | Series:
The museum of phobias | Includes index.
Identifiers: ISBN 9781538259986 (pbk.) | ISBN 9781538260005
(library bound) | ISBN 9781538259993 (6 pack)
Subjects: LCSH: Phobias–Juvenile literature.
Classification: LCC RC535.W66 2021 | DDC 616.85'225–dc23

First Edition

Published in 2021 by
Gareth Stevens Publishing
111 East 14th Street, Suite 349
New York, NY 10003

© 2021 Booklife Publishing
This edition is published by arrangement with Booklife Publishing

Written by: John Wood
Edited by: Madeline Tyler
Designed by: Danielle Jones

All rights reserved. No part of this book may be reproduced in any
form without permission in writing from the publisher, except by a
reviewer.

Printed in the United States of America

CPSIA compliance information: Batch #CS20GS: For further information contact Gareth
Stevens, New York, New York at 1-800-542-2595.

IMAGE CREDITS

Cover – Jiri Hera, schankz, MAHATHIR MOHD YASIN, Alexander Raths, TRAI-MAK, Fer Gregory, fotoslaz. 4 – studiolaska, Julien Hautcoeur. 5 – TheBlackRhino, Dan Ross. 6 – See page for author [CC BY 4.0 (https://creativecommons.org/licenses/by/4.0)], Melkor3D, Authentic travel, ju_see. 7 – Evgeniia Litovchenko, Francey, OneSmallSquare. 8 – Merydolla, Andre Nitsievsky, BaanTaksinStudio. 9 – vhpicstock. 10 – SweetLeMontea, chaossv, Chad Zuber. 11 – SERASOOT. 12 – lineartestpilot, Sebastian Kaulitzki, Kateryna Kon. 13 – Giovanni Cancemi. 14 – lineartestpilot, Nicoleta Ionescu, Glebova Galina. 15 – Shevs. 16 – Bachkova Natalia, lineartestpilot, Andrey_Popov, Gts. 17 – Kzenon. 18 – Art Painter, krungchingpixs, Lefteris Papaulakis, Vitalii Fidyk Photography. 19 – Rachata Teyparsit. 20 – David Peterlin, lineartestpilot, Jeff Baumgart. 21 – Robert Adrian Hillman. 22 – USMC Archives [CC BY 2.0 (https://creativecommons.org/licenses/by/2.0)], Falon Koontz, Hayk_Shalunts. 23 – U.S. army photographer David Conover's shot [Public domain], meunierd. 24 – Tomasz Klejdysz, Andrey_Popov, Cherkas. 25 – Lapina, HHelene. 26 – Sergey Mironov, Paradise studio, worldion, lineartestpilot, karen roach. 27 – dedMazay, nito. 28 – Susse_n, Rawpixel.com, Camila Paez. 29 – Joe Therasakdhi. 30 – MriMan, Viaceslav K. 31 – fizkes, UfaBizPhoto. Images are courtesy of Shutterstock.com. With thanks to Getty Images, Thinkstock Photo and iStockphoto.

The Museum of
PHOBIAS

CONTENTS

WELCOME TO THE

MUSEUM

Come in, come in. We haven't had a visitor to this museum in a long, long time. You must be feeling very brave.

We all know what fear feels like. Our hearts race, our legs shake, and we might feel sick. However, many of us get very afraid of certain things that are not frightening to most other people. These fears are called phobias. Dealing with phobias is not an easy thing to do.

Having a phobia is more than being a bit scared. Phobias are serious fears of something, even if there is no real danger. Phobias can have a big effect on people's lives.

Nobody is exactly sure why we have phobias. Why do they happen? Where do these fears come from? We can have phobias of almost anything, as you will soon find out.

All the things you see in this museum were sent in from people around the world. These phobias are real. Are you ready to walk through these rooms and understand a little bit more about what scares people the most?

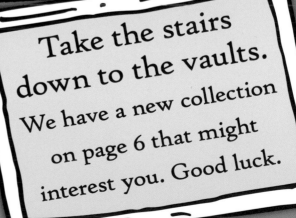

Take the stairs down to the vaults. We have a new collection on page 6 that might interest you. Good luck.

Wiccaphobia

noun

(wik – uh – foh – bee – ah)

Some people say you can hear cackling laughter at night.

It comes from the woods. The people say it is a witch. Somewhere, among those gnarled trees, she practices a dark, powerful magic. She collects all sorts of strange, disgusting ingredients for her spells – the eye of a toad, the blood of a goat, and a single hair from a child's head. Maybe she lives in a cave and only comes out at night. What old, evil magic is she creating? Just the thought of her, deep underground and alone, makes you scared. You feel nervous and you start to sweat. This is wiccaphobia, the fear of witches.

Nowadays, witches are thought to have big black hats, warts on their skin, and broomsticks that fly.

A group of witches is called a coven.

6

One of the most famous witch hunts happened from 1692 to 1693 in a North American village called Salem. It was called the Salem Witch Trials, and 150 people were said to be witches. Nineteen were killed and five died in prison.

Wiccaphobia
The fear of witches

Pogonophobia

noun

(pog – on – uh – foh – bee – ah)

Maybe you have seen a man with a beard before.

Was it your dad or your uncle? Your teacher? Did they have a dark, tangled beard or were the hairs thin and tough, like little wires? When you looked at them, did you feel a twinge of fear? Some people do. Some are afraid of all the germs and dirt and crumbs hidden away between the hairs. Others are scared because they cannot see the bearded person's face. Who are they? What are they hiding? Your breathing gets faster and you start to worry. This is pogonophobia, the fear of beards.

In ancient Egypt, beards were a sign of power. The rulers of ancient Egypt, called pharaohs, wore fake beards.

Some people are also scared of short beards, or any hair on the lower part of the face.

The longest beard belonged to a man called Hans Langseth. When he died in 1927, it was over 17.5 feet (5.3 m) long. That is longer than the height of most giraffes.

Pogonophobia
The fear of beards

Genuphobia

noun

(jen – yoo – foh – bee – ah)

It is a sunny day at the beach.

Most people would be feeling relaxed and happy, but not everyone. Maybe you are one of the few people who would be shivering and shaking at the sight of rows and rows of knees. At the beach, everyone gets their shorts and swimsuits on, and there is nowhere to hide from their knees. You can't explain the fear, but it is there. Whether the knees are bony or big, bruised or lopsided, you feel sick to your stomach. The thought of touching these odd little body parts fills you with dread. This is genuphobia, the fear of knees.

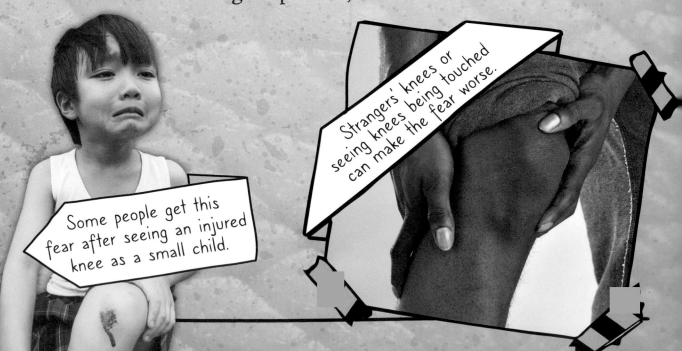

Some people get this fear after seeing an injured knee as a small child.

Strangers' knees or seeing knees being touched can make the fear worse.

People with genuphobia might be afraid of their own knees.

Genuphobia

The fear of knees

SCIENCE CENTER

Nervous System

There are lots of things that happen to your body when you are scared. You might feel hot and sweaty or shake and feel sick. Your breathing and heart rate will get faster. This is all caused by your body's nervous system.

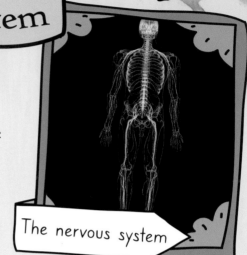

The nervous system

These are the adrenal glands. Glands are special parts of the body that release helpful things.

The nervous system is a network of nerves that send messages. Some messages the brain sends are controlled by you. Some are automatic, such as the messages sent when you are scared. When you are scared, your brain sends a message to the adrenal glands. These glands release something called adrenaline.

Messages from the brain can sometimes travel as fast as 268 miles (431 km) per hour around the body.

ADRENALINE

Adrenaline travels all over your body through the blood. It tells the body parts to get ready for action. Adrenaline is what makes your heart beat faster, your body breathe quicker, and your muscles tense up. Everything is going into overdrive. Your senses become sharper and you will have more energy.

FALSE ALARM

The nervous system is like an alarm. Sometimes this alarm goes off when there is no real danger. This is what is happening when you have a phobia. Your brain thinks that your phobia is dangerous, even if it isn't.

Novercaphobia

noun

(noh – ver – kuh – foh – bee – ah)

She might be strict. She might be strange. She is definitely scary.

For some people, a stepmother can create a deep sense of fear. They worry about this woman taking control of their lives. They imagine this powerful, nasty stepmother looming over them. They might start to fidget and panic at the thought of it. When the stepmother comes home, their mind goes blank and their stomach feels sick. This is novercaphobia, the fear of stepmothers.

Stepmothers are often shown to be wicked or evil in old stories.

The stepmother in a family has not given birth to the children. She is married to the children's father or mother.

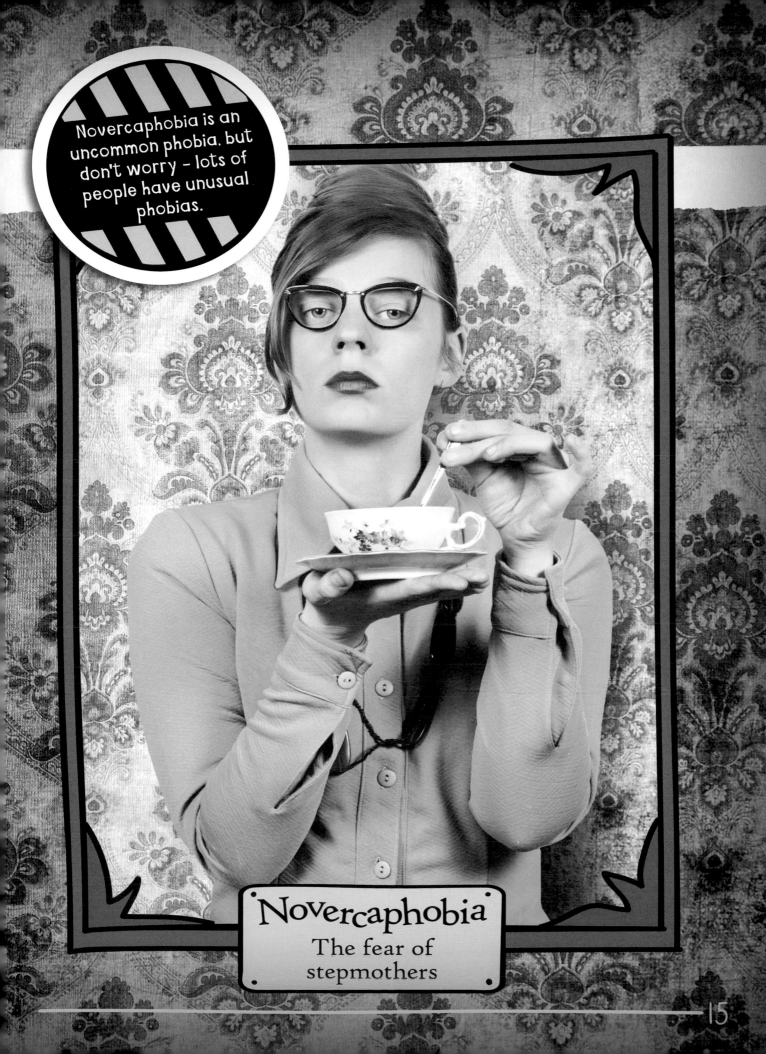

Novercaphobia is an uncommon phobia, but don't worry - lots of people have unusual phobias.

Novercaphobia
The fear of stepmothers

Odontophobia

noun
(oh – don – tuh – foh – bee – ah)

You are waiting your turn outside the dentist's room.

Your stomach feels twisted and your heart is beating quickly. On the other side of that door, people get their teeth pulled out. The dentist tugs and twists till the teeth are wrenched from their soft gums. Even though you know it won't hurt, you still feel scared. Soon you will be in that chair, completely helpless, unable to close your mouth or swallow while the dentist is inches away from your face. Then they will scrape and poke the inside of your mouth. What will they find? What will they take? This is odontophobia, the fear of dentists and teeth.

Odontophobia is the fear of teeth, but it often becomes a fear of going to the dentist too.

When people have odontophobia, they might not go to the dentist. This can create big problems for their teeth.

Going to see the dentist doesn't have to be scary. You'll be taken good care of, and it very rarely hurts.

Odontophobia
The fear of dentists and teeth

Gymnophobia

noun

(jim – noh – foh – bee – ah)

For some people, clothes do more than keep their bodies warm.

For some people, clothes are protection from their greatest fear – being naked. Just the thought of being naked might make some people shake with fear. It might have something to do with how open and helpless we might feel while naked. There is nowhere to hide. Our bodies are private, and being naked leaves us open. You feel the fear rise in your chest. This is gymnophobia, the fear of nakedness.

Throughout history, statues of naked people have sometimes been covered up using fig leaves.

People with gymnophobia might not like to see themselves naked, or they might be afraid of seeing other people naked.

This phobia can make everyday activities, such as showering, very difficult. People who have this fear might also dislike getting changed into different clothes.

Gymnophobia
The fear of nakedness

Glossophobia

noun
(gloss – oh – foh – bee – ah)

Your legs are shaking as you go to the front of the crowd.

Everybody is looking at you. Hundreds of pairs of eyes are fixed on your every movement. Each face is blank, with no emotion. Who knows what these people are thinking? You try to speak, but your throat is dry and the words are stuck. You can feel the weight of their stares pressing against you – it is overpowering, like the glare of the sun. Everyone is waiting for you to say something, but the silence stretches on and on. The soundless seconds feel like hours and each passing moment gets worse. And everyone is still waiting. This is glossophobia, the fear of speaking in front of people.

Being scared of talking in front of crowds is sometimes called stage fright.

This is the 44th president of the U.S., Barack Obama, giving a speech to a big crowd of people.

Glossophobia is more common in younger people than older people.

Glossophobia
The fear of speaking
in front of people

MARILYN MONROE

Marilyn Monroe was a famous actor and model from the U.S. She was born in 1926, and had a very difficult childhood. Her parents weren't able to look after her, so she was brought up in an orphanage.

When Marilyn grew up, she became a model and actor. She starred in 23 films, which altogether earned over $190 million. She became one of the most famous people in the U.S., and many people still know her name now. But Marilyn had a phobia that you might not expect from an actor...

Marilyn's real name was Norma Jeane. She changed it to Marilyn Monroe when she acted in her first film.

Her name can be found on the Hollywood Walk of Fame in Hollywood, California.

MARILYN MONROE

Marilyn's Glossophobia

Marilyn Monroe had a fear of speaking. Growing up, she spoke with a stutter. This meant that she would say the first sound of a word over and over again and found it hard to say the rest. She felt that her throat was paralyzed by fear. Paralyzed means unable to move.

What Did Marilyn Do?

Phobias don't always go away forever, but there are ways to manage them. Marilyn tried speaking very slowly and carefully. Most of the time it worked, and she became famous for her slow way of talking.

It once took Marilyn over 47 tries to say a line properly in a film.

23

Acarophobia

noun
(ak – ah – ruh – foh – bee – ah)

Don't scratch.

Just ignore the itch on your arm. Try to ignore the frantic, maddening itch dancing over your skin. But wait – what if it is a bug? What if this itch is caused by hundreds of tiny creatures burrowing into your skin? You scratch the itch, making the skin raw and red. Now your scalp is itching. Scratch, scratch. Now it is a spot on your back that you can't reach. You feel sweaty and hot as you imagine your body infested, itching. It won't stop. It never stops. You feel afraid of your own body. This is acarophobia, the fear of itching.

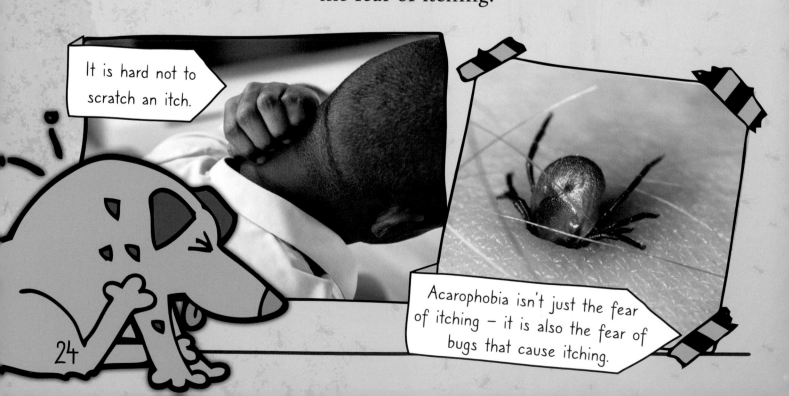

It is hard not to scratch an itch.

Acarophobia isn't just the fear of itching – it is also the fear of bugs that cause itching.

24

People with this phobia might scratch themselves all the time and constantly clean their house.

Acarophobia
The fear of itching

Coulrophobia
noun
(kool – roh – foh – bee – ah)

Step up! Step up! Step right this way! Come and see the stuff of nightmares.

Their faces are as white as skulls. Their noses are as red as blood. And you never know what they are going to do next. Meet the clowns! They will make you laugh until you cry – or maybe you'll just cry. Look at them run around. Aren't they crazy? Look at their strange faces, look at their unnatural smiles. Try to ignore the fear rising in your chest right now, and don't worry about your heartbeat getting faster. This is coulrophobia, the fear of clowns.

Many clowns are covered in bright colors.

Clowns wear makeup.

The idea of clowns has been around for thousands of years. They used to be called jesters, and they would entertain and advise leaders and rulers.

Coulrophobia

The fear of clowns

Phobophobia

noun

(foh – boh – foh – bee – ah)

Why are you here, at this museum?

The curators – the people that have looked after the museum over the years – have all asked themselves the same question. Why did they spend so long collecting and labeling these phobias? You might be wondering what happened to the curators. We don't know either – most of them just disappeared. Maybe they became afraid of... being afraid. Maybe you feel the same way. Does it make you scared when you think about all the phobias you might get? Can you feel the fear creeping into your stomach yet? This is phobophobia, the fear of phobias.

People with phobophobia might be scared of getting other phobias.

Other people with phobophobia might be scared of feeling the signs of fear, such as a tightness in the chest.

Unlike other phobias, worrying about phobophobia can actually bring on the phobia. However, people with this fear can try relaxing exercises, such as slow breathing, yoga, or talking about it with someone.

Phobophobia
The fear of phobias

HELP POINT

Where Do Phobias Come From?

CHILDHOOD EVENTS

Many phobias come from something that happened when people were young. For example, if you meet a very nasty and scary dog, you might think all dogs are terrifying. Young children are still trying to make sense of the world, so their brains make lots of strong connections like this.

LEARNED FROM OTHERS

We might accidentally pick up on signs from other people. For example, if your parents are scared of spiders, they may shout and scream. This can make you want to shout and scream when you see a spider. This is a learned phobia.

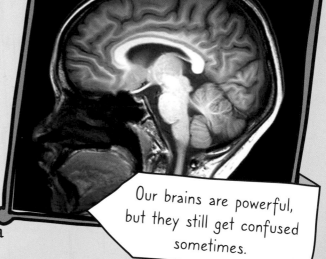

Our brains are powerful, but they still get confused sometimes.

Phobias can be passed on without anybody realizing it.

GENETICS

Genetics has to do with what is passed on from parent to child. There is a genetic code inside every part of our bodies. A genetic code is like a list of instructions on how to make you – for example, what color your hair should be, what shape your face is, or how tall you should be.

Our genetic code is a mixture of our parents' genetic codes. Scientists think that some phobias might come from our genetic code. It gets passed from the parents to their child.

Families usually look like each other because their genetic code is similar.

PHOBIAS CAN MAKE US FEEL:

- Sick
- Shaky
- Sweaty
- Very hot or very cold
- Faint or dizzy
- Out of breath
- As though our heart is beating very fast
- As if we can't think properly or remember the right words

You got to the end. I have to say, I didn't think you could do it.

Maybe you should get something from the gift shop to remember your time here. Or maybe you would rather forget everything you saw today...

INDEX